MASSINAHIGAN SERIES

Brief Accounts of Early Native America

Vol. 1

"You have your Massinahigan*; (that is to say, you have a knowledge of writing), which makes you remember everything."*

— An Algonquin captain to Champlain at Quebec, 1633. The *Jesuit Relations*, Vol. 5, p. 207.

A
BRIEF HISTORY
OF
KING PHILIP'S WAR

1675–1677

Being a Summary of the Articles appearing in the
New-England Historical and Genealogical Register,
from 1883 to 1891, under the title
"Soldiers in King Philip's War."

by

George M. Bodge

Evolution Publishing
Merchantville, New Jersey

Originally printed privately in Boston, 1891. with additional material from:

George Madison Bodge. 1906. *Soldiers in King Philip's War*. Boston.

This edition ©2004, 2024 by Evolution Publishing Merchantville, New Jersey.

Manufactured in the United States of America

Hardcover: ISBN 1-889758-58-2 (2004)
Paperback: ISBN: 978-1-889758-68-8 (2024)

Preface to the 2004 edition

This compact and very readable account is an amalgam of two nearly identical summaries written by George M. Bodge on King Philip's War, a conflict between the New England colonies and the Narraganset and Wampanoag tribes from 1675-1677. It draws from a wealth of primary source material such as New England colonial records, ledgers and unpublished manuscripts, diaries and town records, as well as later historians and local traditions.

Bodge's summary was privately published as a brief pamphlet in 1891, which forms the basis of this present edition. A few additional paragraphs have also been added from the almost identical chapter in Bodge's much larger work, *Soldiers in King Philip's War* (1906). These paragraphs are not in the pamphlet but help to close out the account of the war in sufficient detail.

Readers desiring a more exhaustive account of these events are directed to Bodge's larger work, which includes letters, troop lists, and casualty reports.

—Claudio R. Salvucci, ed.

BRIEF HISTORY OF
KING PHILIP'S WAR.

The sole object of this series of papers was, at the beginning, the preservation in convenient form of the names of those soldiers who served in the Indian War of 1675-7, known as "King Philip's War"; so called from the name of the recognized leader of that war, whose Indian name was Metacom or Pometacom, or Metacomet; but whom the English called Philip. He was the second son of Massasoit, who at the settlement of the English at Plymouth and Boston seems to have been chief sachem of all the various tribes and fragments of tribes living between the Charles River and Narraganset Bay, and including that part of Rhode Island east of the Bay, and also the Cape Cod tribes. The rule of Massasoit was probably rather indefinite both as to limits of territory and extent of authority over the subordinate chiefs. While Massasoit seems to have been the acknowledged head of the tribes within the limits above named, the league between the chiefs of the tribes was evidently very loose, and held mostly for convenience in defence, and perhaps for the settlement of difficulties between individual tribes. The territory of this Sachem was bounded upon the west by the Nipmucks and Narragansets. But a very great proportion of this had been sold by the Sachems before the opening of the war. Massasoit had several children, three of whom are known to us by name; Wamsutta and Metacom, who came to Plymouth about 1656 and at their own request received English names from the Governor, who "christened" them "Alexander" and "Philip." A sister of these was the wife of Tuspaquin, chief of the Namaskets; she was called by the English "Amie." Mention is made of another son and also a daughter, but I have not proper authority for their names. Alexander married a Sachem's daughter, or widow, of the Pocasset tribe, and after his death, soon following Massasoit's, 1661 or '62, she returned to her own people, and ruled there with influence and ability until the war; when her second husband, Petananuet, Petonowowett, or "Peter Nunnuit" (as he is sometimes called), took sides with the English, she, possibly reluctantly, joined the fortunes of Philip, who had married her sister Wootonekanuske, and had great influence with her.

Massasoit had always maintained a cordial and firm friendship with the English; and it would seem that Alexander also was somewhat of his father's nature and disposition. The moment, however, which saw Philip raised to the place of power, gave signal of a far different course of conduct on the part of the Wampanoag Sachem. The limits of his father's olden territory had been greatly reduced before he came to power. The English had purchased and otherwise absorbed a large proportion of their lands. Philip kept on selling and surrendering, till at last, as early as 1670-1, he began to feel the pressure of civilization upon their hunting and fishing grounds as well as cornfields. The Court at Plymouth itself had interfered and forbidden the transfer of certain parts of the Wampanoag territories, and thus doubtless saved the Indians in various tribes a home. Pokanoket, the hereditary home, was thus saved to Philip's people; and here he lived at the time of the opening of the war. This place was called by the English "Mount Hope," and it is now embraced in the town of Bristol, R. I.

But now having given some account of the principal character in the war, we may state briefly the method of collecting the material in these papers, and the purpose of this present pamphlet.

The method adopted in arranging the soldier's names needs explanation. The material which served as the basis of the work, and indeed first suggested the undertaking, was found in three manuscript volumes, containing the accounts of John Hull, who was the Treasurer of the colony at the time of the war. These volumes are devoted to the accounts pertaining to the war, and consist of a Journal and two Ledgers. The Journal was opened June 24th, 1675, and originally contained over five hundred pages, as the Ledger shows, but now has only four hundred and sixty-one complete. There was evidently a later Journal and also a Ledger, now missing, which belonged to the set. The third book is later, and contains the closing accounts in the war. These old books were preserved in private hands for a century and a half, until discovered by one who appreciated their value for genealogy and history, and secured them for those purposes. In searching these books for the name of one who served in the Indian war, the present writer discovered the importance of the accounts in the matter of the Indian war of 1675. Every soldier who served in that war is credited with military service, and the name of the officer under whom he served is given in the credit. The date at which payment is made is given in the 'Cash,' account, but the time and place of service is not designated; nor is the residence nor any further information about the soldier given. Some of the soldiers served at different times and under different officers. The best method therefore of arranging the men in companies was found to be that of following the names of the officers as they occur in the credits. The names were thus gathered from the Journal, and placed in companies with their officers. Then the fortunes of each company were followed as carefully as possible throughout the several campaigns of the war. But it was found that a great amount of unpublished material is still preserved in our State Archives, County and Town Records, and elsewhere; and this, in the light of the great number of names identified in these credits as soldiers, becomes available and interesting as history. Additional material has been gathered and incorporated here from all sources, whenever it would add to the sum of knowledge concerning the war.

The officer and soldiers, many of them, served in several, some in all the different campaigns; and thus in following their fortunes, it was necessary to go over the same events many times, so as to marshal the various companies in order in the military operations. It will be seen that by this method of arrangement, a great amount of important material has been massed together conveniently for the study of history, while the story of the war has not been followed by consecutive events, but according to the experience of individual officers and companies. It is proposed in this introductory chapter to give a brief account of the war, following events in order as nearly as possible. It will not be necessary to discuss the causes leading up to the war. It is enough to say here, that the English had assumed the government of the country, and followed their course of settlement with small regard to the rights of the natives. In some of the plantations, the settlers purchased their lands of the Indians, as a matter of precaution; partly that they might have that show of title in case any other claim should be set up in opposition to theirs, and partly to conciliate the savages, whose hostility they feared, and whose friendship was profitable in the way of trade, in furs and other products of the hunt. The Indians were always at disadvantage with the English, in all the arts of civilized life. The English paid no heed to Indian laws or customs or traditions; and ruthlessly imposed their own laws, customs and religious ideas, with no apparent thought of their intolerance and injustice. They made treaties with the savages in the same terms which they would have used had they been dealing with a civilized nation. They made out deeds, in language which only the learned framers themselves could understand. In brief, the Pilgrims and Puritans mostly looked upon the Indians as heathen, whose "inheritance" God meant to give to his people, as of old he had dealt with Israel and their heathen. There were some, however, who, with Rev. John Eliot, believed that the Indians had immortal souls, and that they were given to God's people to educate and save. But there was nothing which the rulers of the Indians resented more persistently, nor complained of more frequently, than the attempts of the Christians to convert their people. Indirectly one of these converted Indians was the immediate cause of the opening of hostilities. There were many grievances of which the Indians complained; but they had not the foresight to see the inevitable result of the constantly increasing power of the English, in their acquisition of land, and multiplying of settlements. It was only when they felt the pressure of actual privation or persecution, that they began to think of opposition or revenge. Their chiefs had been summoned frequently before the English courts to answer for some breach of law by their subjects; several times the English had demanded that whole tribes should give up their arms because of the fault of one or a few. The Indians lived mostly by hunting and fishing, and at the time of the war used fire-arms almost wholly. They had learned their use and bought the arms of the English, nearly always at exorbitant prices. They were expert in the use of their guns, and held them as the most precious of their possessions. The order to give these over to the English, with their stock of ammunition, was regarded by them as robbery, as indeed in most cases it was, as they seldom regained their arms when once given up. We can now see that from their standpoint there were grievances enough to drive them to rebellion.

But our forefathers seem to have been unable to see any but their own side. But now to the story.

John Sassamon (Mr. Hubbard says Sausaman) was the son of a Wampanoag Indian who with his wife and family lived in Dorchester. They had been taught by Mr. Eliot, and professed the Christian faith. The son John was the pupil of Mr. Eliot from his early youth, and was made a teacher among the Christian Indians at Natick. Mr. Hubbard says that "upon some misdemeanor" there, he went to the Wampanoags. where he became the secretary and interpreter of the chief, to whom he was a most valuable assistant and trusted adviser. He was soon prevailed upon by Mr. Eliot to return to Natick, where he became a preacher, while still preserving friendly relations with Philip and his tribe. In 1672-3 he was at Namasket as preacher among the Indians, whose chief was Tuspaquin, whose daughter Sassamon had married. While here he discovered that a plot was in process, extending among many tribes, to exterminate or drive away the English settlers from the country. This plot Sassamon disclosed to the authorities at Plymouth, and afterwards the story was told to the Massachusetts authorities; and

Philip was summoned to answer to the charge. At the examination, where nothing positive could be proved against Philip, he found by the evidence that Sassamon had betrayed him, and he immediately condemned him to death in his council. The sentence was carried out January 29, 1674–5 while Sassamon was fishing through the ice upon Assawomset Pond. His executioners were brought to punishment, and it was discovered that the deed was done by Philip's order. The trial was in March, 1675, and the principal actor, Tobias, and his accomplice, Mattashunannamoo, were executed as murderers, June 8, 1675; while Tobias's son, who was present but took no part in the crime, was reprieved for one month and then shot. After the execution of the two in June, Philip threw off all disguise as to his plan, and pushed his preparations as diligently as possible. The plan had been to complete preparations and include all the tribes in New England, so that a simultaneous assault could he made upon all the settlements at once. This plan was spoiled, and probably the settlements saved from destruction, by the impatience of the leader's vengeance. While Philip's preparations went forward; the authorities thought best not to make any immediate military demonstration further than the placing of a guard by the various settlements to prevent a surprise. They thought Philip would soon tire of holding his men in arms and training, so that they could get him in their power. But his company increased, and the younger warriors began to demand some open act of hostility. At last they began not only to insult the English settlers in the nearest settlements, by their words of insolence and threats, but to shoot their cattle and plunder their houses. The Indians increased greatly in numbers, from the neighboring tribes, many "strange Indians" appearing among them, and most of their women and children being sent away to the Narraganset country. At Swansy they appeared in considerable numbers, and used all their ways of provocation to induce some act of resistance from the settlers; and at last, upon June 24th, one man was so enraged at the shooting of his cattle and the attempt to rifle his house, that he shot at an Indian, wounding him. Upon this the Indians began open and indiscriminate hostility, and on that day eight or nine of the English at Swansy were killed and others wounded. Two men were sent for a surgeon but were waylaid and slain, and their bodies left upon the road. Messengers, sent from the English authorities to treat with Philip and prevent an outbreak, came upon the bodies of the men slain in the highway, and speedily turned back. The colonies awoke to the fact that an Indian war was upon them, but supposed that a few companies sent down to Swansy would at once overawe the savages and reduce them to submission. A speedy muster was made, both at Plymouth and Boston, and on the afternoon of June 26th, five companies were mustering or on the march from the two colonies. The details of the account of the war will be found in the body of the preceding chapters. Here only a brief outline of current events can be given. The first company of infantry from Boston was made up from the regular military companies of the town. A company of cavalry, or "troopers," was gathered from the regular organization in three counties. A third company, of "volunteers," was raised about the town and vicinity, from all sorts of adventurers, sea-faring men and strangers, with a number of prisoners who had been convicted of piracy and condemned to death, but were now released to engage in fighting the Indians. Capt. Daniel Henchman commanded the first company; Capt. Thomas Prentice the troopers, and Capt. Samuel Mosely the "volunteers." These three companies marched out of Boston on the 26th and 27th and arrived at Swansy on the 28th, having formed a junction with the Plymouth forces under Major James Cudworth and Capt. Fuller. The forces quartered about the house of Rev. John Miles, the minister at Swansy, whose place was nearest the bridge leading over the river into Philip's dominions. Some of the troopers that evening rode across the bridge and had a slight skirmish with the enemy. On the 29th, Major Thomas Savage arrived with another company of foot with Capt. Nicholas Paige's troop. Major Savage took command of the Massachusetts forces; while, according to the custom in the United Colonies, the senior officer of the colony in which the forces were engaged at the time became commander-in-chief The present seat of war being in Plymouth colony, Major Cudworth was thus the commander of the whole army. On June 30th, the troopers, supported by Mosely's company, charged across the bridge for a mile into the woods, driving the enemy before them into swamps, with a loss of five or six, Ensign Perez Savage being severely wounded on the English side. This charge so frightened the Indians that they fled, in the night out of their peninsula of Mount Hope, across the channel to Pocasset, now Tiverton, R. I., so that on the next day when the whole force marched over into Mount Hope, and marched back and forth sweeping the country with their lines, they found no enemy. The forces were engaged several days in scouting the neighboring country in search of the Indians, not yet knowing that the main body were in Pocasset.

Then orders came from Boston for Major Savage's forces to march into Narraganset, to enforce a treaty with that powerful tribe, and prevent their junction with Philip. They found the country apparently deserted, few except the very aged being left in any of the villages. Neither Canonchet nor any of his leading Sachems could be found. The officers, however, spent several days completing a very ceremonious treaty with some of the old men whom they were able to bring together. Canonchet afterwards treated the whole matter with scorn as being a farce.

In the meantime the Plymouth forces passed over to Pocasset and found a body of Indians, and had a skirmish with them. Capt. Fuller was in command, and Benjamin Church conducted a part of the force which became engaged with a much larger force, and after hard fighting were drawn off with difficulty by the tact and courage of Mr. Church, after inflicting serious injury upon the enemy, and suffering little loss themselves. After this the Indians retired into the swamps about Pocasset, and were held at bay until the return of the Massachusetts forces; when all marched together for concerted action against their enemies.

On July 18th the combined forces arrived at the Pocasset swamp, and made a resolute attack upon the enemy concealed in the thick underbrush, from whence at the first volley they killed five and wounded seven of our men. After this volley the enemy retreated deeper into the swamp, where it was impossible, night coming on, to follow them. The commanders in council concluded that they had the enemy now enclosed securely within the swamp, whence it was impossible to escape, if a suitable guard were left to watch. Major Savage and the Massachusetts men returned to Boston, except Capt. Henchman's company of one hundred men, who, with the Plymouth forces, remained at Pocasset. Capt. Henchman began to build a fort there, which might serve as a stronghold for the English and might guard the entrance to the great swamp.

The English were deceived by the apparent easy conquest of both the Wampanoags and Narragansets, and believed they had overawed them and set their hostility at rest, and now might take their own time in crushing Philip and thus finishing the war.

Plymouth Colony had been engaged from the first in seeking to conciliate the tribes, in their bounds, which were related to Philip. Through the efforts of Mr. Benjamin Church, a resident of Seconet, who was acquainted on pleasant terms with nearly all the tribes in the colony; negotiations were held with Awashonks the squaw-sachem of the Seconet Indians and Weetamoo the squaw-sachem or "queen" of the Pocasset tribe. Awashonks and most of her people passed over into the Narraganset country at the opening of active hostilities, and thus avoided joining Philip; but Weetamoo and her people were swept along with him in his retreat towards the Nipmuck country. Plymouth companies were abroad, too, scouting the country in the effort to protect their settlements, exposed, like Dartmouth, Middleboro, &c. They also established a garrison at Mount Hope after Philip retreated to Pocasset, to prevent his return. The entrance of Philip into the Pocasset swamps compelled the coöperation of the hesitating Weetamoo, and afforded him a safe hiding-place to recruit and prepare for his flight northward.

In the meantime the Massachusetts authorities had begun negotiations with the various Nipmuck Indians. Seven of the principal towns had been visited and treaties made with each. On July 16th Ephraim Curtis returned to Boston and reported the Quabaugs gathered at a great Island in a swamp beyond Brookfield, and showing a defiant and hostile spirit. The Council immediately sent Capt. Edward Hutchinson, escorted by Capt. Thomas Wheeler and his mounted company, with Curtis as guide, to find the Indians and bring them to terms. The company, accompanied by some friendly Naticks, arrived at Brookfield on August 1st, and immediately sent Curtis with the guides to arrange for a meeting next day. The Quabaugs, whose leader was the famous Muttaump, agreed to come next day to a plain some three miles from Brookfield to meet the English. The next morning, the company, with three of the chief men of Brookfield, rode out to the appointed place, but found no Indians. Urged by the Brookfield men, but against the earnest remonstrance of the Naticks, they rode forward towards the place where Curtis met them the day before. But coming to a narrow defile between a high rocky hill and an impenetrable swamp, and riding single file, they found themselves caught in a great ambuscade of the Indians, who let them pass along until they were able to surround them, and then rose altogether and fired into their column at close range. They killed eight men outright and wounded five, including Capts. Hutchinson and Wheeler, the former mortally. The English were forced to retreat, fighting, up the hill; and, under the skilful conduct of their Indian guides, were able to make a safe retreat to Brookfield where they gathered the people and fortified a house just before the Indians came sweeping furiously down upon the village. Here they defended themselves against great numbers for several days, till Major Willard and Capt. Parker came with a company and reinforced the garrison, when the enemy retired.

At Pocasset, Capt. Henchman continued building his fort, and Philip was making ready for his flight. The English seem not to have contemplated the possibility of a general war, nor to have at all appreciated the gravity of the present situation in the colonies. Philip with all his fighting-men and the greater part of his own and Weetamoo's people, escaped across the river and passed through the open plain in Rehoboth, where they were discovered by some of the settlers. A scouting party from Taunton made the discovery that it was Philip's Indians who were thus escaping. The situation of affairs may be briefly stated. Capt. Henchman was guarding the swamp wherein Philip and his people were supposed to be securely trapped. Major Cudworth and Capt. Fuller were at Dartmouth with a company of one hundred and twelve men. Lieut. Nathaniel Thomas of Marshfield was at the Mount Hope garrison with twenty men. At Rehoboth a company of Mohegan Indians under Oneko, under convoy of

Corporal Thomas Swift, arrived from Boston on the 30th on their way to Capt. Henchman at Pocasset. Upon the alarm, Rev. Mr. Newman, of Rehoboth, began to organize a company of volunteers for the pursuit of the Indians. Lieut. Thomas, with a small detachment, happened to come to Rehoboth on the 30th, and hearing of the escape, hastened back to carry the news to Capt. Henchman, and urge his coöperation. Lieut. Thomas then, on the 31st, took eleven men of his Mount Hope garrison, and being joined by Lieut. James Brown, of Swansy, with twelve men, marched in the pursuit. The Rehoboth men, with some volunteers from Providence and Taunton, led by the Mohegans, had started earlier upon the trail of the enemy. Lieut. Thomas and his party overtook the others at sunset, and after a brief council-of-war, sent out their scouts, Indian and English, to discover the movements of the fugitives. Having found that they had encamped for the night, and apparently not suspecting pursuit, the English left their horses with a guard, and, with the Mohegans in the van, marched silently forward to a field, at a place called "Nipsachick" (said to be within the present town of Burrillville,

RI.). The night being very dark, they were forced to wait for light. At dawn they made their attack upon what proved to be Weetamoo's camp. The Indians were taken by surprise and fled, leaving everything behind them. But the Mohegans and English rushing forward found themselves confronted with Philip's fighting men entrenched behind trees and rocks ready for battle. Adopting the tactics of the enemy, the English and their allies engaged them fiercely until 9 o'clock, when still fighting desperately, but with powder nearly spent, the hostiles sullenly retired, leaving many of their dead upon the field. Some twenty-three of the enemy were killed, it is said, including a prominent chief, Woonashum, called by the English, Nimrod. Of the English, two were killed and one wounded.

Near the close of the fight, Rev. Mr. Newman and a party came up, bringing supplies. Capt. Henchman arrived after the fight, having sailed to Providence and marched up thence, with sixty-eight soldiers and sixteen friendly Indians. He immediately took command, but concluded not to push the pursuit until next day. The Rehoboth and Providence men returned home, to bring up supplies for the further pursuit. They hastened back next day with all speed, but found to their great disappointment that Capt. Henchman had not moved until that same day, giving the enemy a full day's start; and Lieut. Thomas and his party overtook him on the evening of August 3d, at a place called by them in the report, "Wapososhequash." The enemy were beyond pursuit, a part (Weetamoo's people, except the fighting-men) having turned off into the Narraganset country, while Philip and the rest passed into the great forests beyond Quabaug. The Mohegans went to their own country on August 4th, accompanied by Lieut. Brown and a small party, to Norwich, to secure provisions and news of the enemy. After awaiting the return of this party three days, Capt. Henchman on August 7th, marched back to Mendon, meeting Capt. Mosely with a company of dragoons coming up from Providence with supplies. Next day Capt. Henchman went up to Boston, and the Rehoboth men returned home. Capt. Mosely was left in command at Mendon. Capt. Henchman was relieved of command in the field and was sent to bring off his men remaining at Pocasset. Mendon had been attacked July 14th, by a party of Nipmucks, led by Matoonas, and six or more of the settlers were killed while at work in their fields.

When the Indians returned from their siege of Brookfield, they met Philip and his people in the woods and told him of their exploit. He was greatly pleased, and gave some of the chiefs presents of wampum, and promised them fresh supplies of ammunition and arms. The Brookfield affair had the effect of bringing in the faltering tribes, and Philip's coming confirmed the plan to clear the Connecticut Valley of English settlers. Massachusetts Colony raised several companies to protect the frontiers. Capt. Mosely with his own and Capt. Henchman's men marched from Mendon, and Capts. Thomas Lathrop of Essex County with a fine company, and Richard Beers of Watertown with another, marched to Brookfield where their forces were joined by Capt. Watts of Connecticut with two companies of English and Indians. Major Willard took command of this force, and broke it into several parties in order to better protect the several settlements. These companies were engaged in scouting the frontiers and guarding supplies sent up to the various garrisons. The Springfield Indians, hitherto pretending friendship, fled and joined the hostiles on the night of August 24; and the English, pursuing, had a sharp fight with them at a swamp near Mt. Wequomps, losing nine of their own men. The English troops were concentrated at Hadley under the general command of Major Pynchon. On Sept. 1st the Indians attacked Deerfield, burning most of the houses and killing one of the garrison soldiers, and withdrew. On the 2d they fell upon Northfield, where many of the people were abroad at work in the fields, and the women and children at the houses in the town. The assault was from all quarters at once, and many were killed in the fields and as they escaped from their houses to the garrison. The Indians burned most of their houses and drove away their cattle. On the 3d, Capt. Beers, with thirty mounted men and an ox-team, was sent to bring off the garrison of Northfield, not knowing of this attack. This force on the next day was ambushed at Saw-Mill Brook, near Northfield, and Capt. Beers and some twenty of his men were killed. Next day Major Treat with a hundred men marched up to Northfield, finding and burying the dead of Capt. Beers's company, and then bringing off the garrison. It was now decided to strengthen the garrisons and act upon the defensive. Upon Sept. 18th Capt. Lathrop with his company was sent to convoy teams bringing loads of grain from Deerfield to Hadley. A strong ambuscade was made at a place known since as "Bloody Brook," and there the Indians encompassed and massacred nearly the whole company, some eighty, including the teamsters. Only eight or ten escaped. The number killed was between sixty and seventy. Capt. Mosely came hastily from Deerfield upon hearing the shots, and engaged the great company of several hundreds of Indians, charging in amongst them with intrepid fury which drove them headlong before him into the woods and swamps; but, finding them gathering in immense numbers and seeking to surround him, he threw out his lines to prevent being flanked, and began a cautious retreat; when Major Treat coming upon the field, the Indians, seeing the reinforcements, fled.

These terrible reverses threw a gloomy, superstitious fear over the colonies. The English troops, hitherto despising the Indians in war, now seemed helpless before them. On Sept. 26th the Indians assaulted Springfield, west of the river, burning the houses and barns. On October 5th, having made some demonstrations against Hadley, the soldiers were drawn from Springfield to strengthen the garrison; the Indians fell upon the latter village and destroyed it, before the companies could return to save it. After this blow, Major Pynchon begged the Court to appoint a commander of the forces on the river in his place, and Major Samuel Appleton was appointed, and by advice of the Council garrisoned the various towns not abandoned, and then withdrew the other troops to Boston. The Connecticut troops helped to garrison Northampton and Westfield, and the Indians withdrew to their winter camps. Philip had long since gone into winter quarters above Albany.

But now the colonies determined to strike the Narragansets in their own country before they should be able to join the hostiles. A great muster was made in three colonies, and an army of one thousand men was raised and equipped, half of which was sent from Massachusetts. The Narragansets were entrenched in a very strong position in a great swamp in what is now South Kingstown, R. I. It was claimed that great numbers of Wampanoags and other hostiles were among them finding refuge, and they were defiant and threatening. The English forces under command of Gen. Winslow of Plymouth gathered at Wickford, and on December 19th, 1675, marched some twenty miles through intense cold and a heavy snow-storm, to the swamp; the waters had been frozen by the severe cold, and this fact made it possible for the English to reach the rude fortifications. Without waiting for any organized attack, the Massachusetts troops, being at the front in the march, rushed forward across the ice in an impetuous charge, and into the entrance, where the Indians had constructed rude flankers, and placed a strong block-house in front, so that the first to enter were met with a terrible enfilading fire from front and flanks, and were forced back for a time; but others coming on pressed into the breach, and, though suffering severe losses, at last stormed all the fortifications, drove the enemy from every line of entrenchments within the fort, and out into the woods and swamps beyond. They set fire to the wigwams and store-houses of the savages, in which were burned many of the aged, and women and children. Then taking their wounded, the English took up their march back through the deep snow to Wickford, where they arrived the next morning.

The details of this fight, as well as the subsequent movements of this campaign, are given at length in the articles of which this pamphlet is the compendium, and are briefly passed here. The Narragansets kept well out of the way of the English army, and made many pretences of negotiating peace, but at last, about January 26th, having made several raids into the settlements, and captured numbers of cattle and horses, Canonchet with his strong rear-guard took up his line of retreat for the north, and two days afterwards the army, some twelve hundred strong, marched in pursuit. The Mohegans and Pequots, among the Connecticut forces, led the pursuit, and had several sharp skirmishes with the enemy, always retreating northward. This running fight was kept up for several days, until provisions having failed and no base of supplies possible, the General abandoned the pursuit and marched his troops to Marlborough and thence to Boston. The men suffered severely in this march, from hunger, and it was known for several generations as the "hungry march."

The Connecticut forces separated from the others on February 3d, and the main body of the army arrived in Boston on the 8th and were dismissed. A company under command of Capt. Wadsworth was left at Marlborough to guard the frontiers and neighboring towns. Canonchet and his great and warlike Narraganset tribe, maddened by what they believed their wrongs, and thirsting for vengeance, were now joined with Philip and the other hostile tribes, and all within an easy day's call, except Philip and his band who still remained in their retreat beyond Albany. The time was critical for the settlements; prompt action was necessary on the part of the Indian leaders, to keep their young men in courage and training. Upon February 10th the Indians in great force fell upon Lancaster, and nearly destroyed the town. They killed or took captive fifty of the people. Among the captives was Mrs. Rowlandson, wife of the minister. One garrison-house was saved by the arrival of Capt. Wadsworth and his company from Marlborough. On February 21st a strong body of the enemy surprised Medfield, although a large force of soldiers was then in the town. There were no guards set, nor other precautions taken. The soldiers were scattered about in the houses, and the Indians placed ambuscades in front of each house, and shot them down as they rushed out upon the alarm. The enemy were frightened away by the firing of a cannon, and crossed the river, burning the bridge behind them. Another army was now raised and sent out to the Connecticut River towns, to protect them, and try to bring the enemy to battle. There were said to be two great fortified camps; one near the "Wachusett Hill," and the other at Menameset, beyond Brookfield. The army was under command of Major Thomas Savage, and consisted of three foot companies and a troop of horse from Massachusetts. Connecticut sent several companies of English and friendly Indians. A number of Christian Indians from the Naticks went with Major Savage. The army marched to Menameset, March 2d–4th, to find the enemy gone. They pursued them to Miller's River, across which they escaped. It was thought that this great body of the enemy would now fall upon the Western towns, so that the army marched thither, abandoning the design upon "Wachusett Hill" encampment. Major Savage disposed his forces to guard the towns. On

March 14th an attack was made upon Northampton, but was repulsed with severe loss to the enemy. On the 24th they appeared at Hatfield, but finding it well garrisoned made no attack, though driving off some horses and cattle. The Indians began to prepare for planting fields along the river; and Canonchet with a body of his men went back to their country to bring up seed-corn of which large quantities were there stored. It is probable that a large company went towards Plymouth colony, a small party of whom destroyed the house and family of Mr. Clarke at Plymouth village. March 17th they burned Warwick. Plymouth Colony sent out a company of fifty under Capt. Michael Peirse of Marshfield, to protect its frontiers. A party of twenty friendly Indians under "Capt. Amos" was joined with Capt. Peirse. This company marched to Seekonk, and there had a sharp skirmish with the Indians on the evening of March 25th. Next day, supposing they had beaten the Indians, they pursued them and were drawn into an ambush and surrounded near Patuxit River with great numbers, so that they were obliged to fight to the death. The whole company, including the officers, were killed, together with eight out of the twenty Indians. The enemy, too, lost very heavily. March 28th and 29th the Indians burned seventy houses and thirty barns at Providence.

In the meantime in Massachusetts the enemy were not idle. Lurking parties hovered about Groton, plundering the vacated houses, and driving away any stray cattle within safe reach. On March 13th they fell upon the town in force. The people were gathered in five garrison-houses. One of the garrison-houses was captured, but the people mostly escaped to another. The other garrison-houses were stoutly defended. The Indians burned the unfortified houses and withdrew. On March 26th, the fatal day of Capt. Peirse's destruction, they burned sixteen houses and thirteen barns at Marlborough. Capt. Brocklebank, then in command at Marlborough, sent out a party in pursuit, who overtook and surprised the enemy at night sleeping about their fires, fired into their midst and put them to flight. On the same day, at Longmeadow, a party going to Springfield to church was ambushed by a small company of Indians, and several were captured and killed.

Finding the campaign to have failed in its main object, the Council ordered Major Savage to withdraw his troops, leaving Capt. Wm. Turner, with a hundred and fifty men, to garrison the towns. April 7th the army marched homeward.

But now the Connecticut authorities, fearing a return of the Narragansets to their vicinity, in numbers such as overwhelmed Capt. Peirse, mustered a mixed company of English and Indians, and sent them into the Narraganset country under command of Capts. Denison and Avery. These, guided by a captive whom they had taken, surprised and captured Canonchet not far from the Patuxit river, where he was encamped with a few of his men, while the great body were scattered, scouting and foraging. He was soon after executed by Oneko, by the judgment of the English authorities. The death of Canonchet was really the death-blow of the war, for he was the real leader of all active operations at this time. Philip was still the chief instigator, however, and now more than before, became, for the time, the controlling mind of a larger number than ever before. There were dissensions, however, and many of the chiefs began to murmur and some to threaten against him as the cause of all their troubles. Some of the river tribes began to show signs of weakening, and proposed negotiations with the English. Philip withdrew to the strong-hold near Wachuset with such as adhered to him, and with Quinnapin, and such of the Narragansets as followed him. The Indians were still active, and watched every chance to strike a blow. They came to Marlborough on April 18th and burned the abandoned houses of the settlers. Capt. Brocklebank commanded the garrison there and refused to be drawn out into the ambuscades, which, before the burning, the Indians had set. On April 20th they crept down and encompassed the town of Sudbury. On that day Capt. Wadsworth marched up from Boston with a company of fifty men, passed through Sudbury, and doubtless the lines of the enemy, without any knowledge of their vicinity. He was forcing his march to relieve the garrison at Marlborough, where they arrived about midnight on the 20th, and without delay leaving their recruits, took those relieved to come home, including Capt. Brocklebank, and came back towards Sudbury. The great numbers of Indians had encompassed the town, and in the morning of the

21st began to burn outlying houses, to draw out the inhabitants from the garrison. They soon made a furious and persistent attack on Haines's garrison from morning till mid-day, but were beaten off, until rumors of reinforcements from various quarters caused them to withdraw to meet these. Edward Cowen and eighteen troopers coming to the relief of Sudbury were attacked, but escaped with only four killed, they turned back, suspecting the ambush laid for them. Capt. Wadsworth soon after arrived by another road, and meeting with an outpost of the enemy rushed forward to engage them, and, as usual, they soon found themselves surrounded by great numbers, and were forced to a position on a hill, where most of the company fell fighting, including Capts. Wadsworth, Brockle-bank and Lieut. Sharpe. Some sixteen of the company managed to escape to a mill, and there defended themselves until relieved. A company from Watertown arrived soon after Capt. Wads-worth, and crossing the river, made a brave attempt to get to the hill to join him in his desperate fight, but were nearly surrounded themselves and forced to retire. Capt. Hunting with a company of Christian Indians and a squad of troopers arrived from Charlestown late in the afternoon, in time to rescue the men at the mill. After this fight, in which they struck such a terrible blow, and so close to Boston, too, they seem to have retired to their several camps, and soon to have gathered to their great fishing-places in order to take the run of fish. Capt. Turner was still in command of the garrisons at the west. From captives who had escaped, and scouts here and there, came rumors of a great company of Indians fishing at the "Upper Falls" of the Connecticut. Capt. Turner and his officers were anxious to strike a blow against the enemy, and Connecticut authorities were applied to, and promised speedy reinforcements. On May 12th the Indians made a raid into Deerfield meadows and stampeded some seventy head of cattle belonging to the English. Roused by this fresh outrage, the people urged retaliation, and Capt. Turner and his officers determined to attack the Indians at their great fishing place at once. On May 18th the whole company of soldiers and volunteers, about one hundred and fifty, mustered at Hatfield, and marched out at evening toward the "Falls." They eluded the outposts of the enemy, and at daylight arrived undiscovered at the camp of the Indians at the fishing-place. The savages were asleep in their wigwams, and the English rushed down upon them and shot them by scores, pointing their muskets in through the wigwam doors. No resistance was possible, and those who escaped the first fire fled in terror to the river, pursued by the soldiers and were cut down or driven into the water without mercy; many were drowned attempting to cross the river.

But it was soon found that there were several other great bodies of the Indians, above and below the Falls on both sides of the river, and these began to swarm towards the fight. Capt. Turner now prudently began a retreat, having struck his blow. As the soldiers retired the enemy gathered in great numbers upon rear and flanks, seeking to force the English into narrow defiles. Capt. Holyoke commanded the rear-guard, and checked the enemy by stout fighting, but for which, it is likely, the whole command would have been lost. Capt. Turner led the advance, and while crossing Green River was shot down by Indians lying in wait. Capt. Holyoke then led the company back to Hatfield, fighting nearly the whole way. There the killed and missing numbered forty-five. A few came in afterwards, reducing the number of the lost to about forty. It is estimated that some two hundred Indians must have been destroyed.

The blow struck by Capt. Turner greatly intimidated the enemy, though the retreat was so disastrous to the English. The tribes became divided and demoralized. They seem to have broken up into small wandering parties. Philip with large numbers of his adherents went down towards Plymouth. Massachusetts sent troops to the western frontiers again, and also to aid Plymouth. The operations in the field were mostly the pursuit of non-combatants, the aged, and women and children. Large numbers of the Wampanoags and Narragansets had now returned with Philip to their own country. Small parties from time to time plundered and killed as opportunity offered. The colonists were roused to new activity at the evident weakening of the Indians. Aid was sent to Plymouth, under Capts. Brattle and Mosely; and Capt. Henchman did good service in the parts about Brookfield. Major Talcott, with a mixed force of English and Indians, about five hundred in all, came up the river and marched into Hadley about the 11th of June, and was quartered there on the 12th, when the Western Indians, some seven hundred strong, made their last great assault in force in these parts. The town was quite strongly garrisoned besides this reinforcement, of which probably the enemy knew nothing. The attack was altogether unexpected and was furious and determined, but the repulse was decided and sanguinary. Major Talcott then led his force down into the Narraganset country, where, about the 2d of July, he encountered a great body of Indians, and driving them into the woods and swamps slew great numbers, and took many captives. The plight of the savages was pitiful; without ammunition, without leadership, without country or hope of any sort, they found no mercy now at the hands of their olden foes, the Mohegans and Pequots, nor yet the English.

The remaining operations of the war in these parts were simply the hunting down of almost defenceless enemies. The colonial authorities issued a proclamation, calling all those Indians who had been engaged in the war to come in and surrender, submitting themselves to the judgment of the English courts. Many parties sought to take advantage of this, but were captured upon their approach by scouting parties, and treated as captives. Some of those who had been prominent in the war and could not hope for mercy, escaped to the eastward and put themselves under the protection of Wannalancet and his Pennacooks, who had remained neutral. Some fled further to the east, and there incited war.

The constant success which the Connecticut troops had always had after their use of the Mohegans and Pequots, was a plain rebuke to the Massachusetts colonists for the numerous disasters from which the Christian Indians might have saved them, if they had trusted and employed them. As soon as Capt. Hunting and his Indian company were put in the field, this appeared. The Indians in small parties skulking in woods and swamps might have eluded English soldiers for years, but as soon as other Indians were employed, escape was impossible.

At the close of July, many of Philip's followers had been taken, and his wife and several of his chief men were captives or had been killed. With a small band of his followers he was hiding in the swamps at Mounthope and Pocasset. English scouting parties were active in all parts of the colonies hunting down the trembling and unresisting fugitives; and especially Philip. Benjamin Church was among the most active in hunting and bringing in the Indians, and when one of Philip's men came to betray his chief, he found Mr. Church at Major Sanford's in Rhode Island with his party of English and Indians a short distance away. Upon the news of Philip's hiding-place and the offer of the Indian to lead thither, Mr. Church gathered as many as he could enlist in addition to his party, and, under the lead of the Indian deserter (who acted, it is said from motives of revenge for his brother's death, by Philip's hand, because he advised him to make peace with the English), the party marched with great secrecy to Mounthope. Mr. Church arranged his attack with skill, and came upon Philip's party unguarded and asleep, and Philip springing up and attempting to escape to the swamp near by, was confronted with two of Mr. Church's guards, an Englishman and an Indian. The Englishman's gun missed fire, but the Indian, named "Alderman," immediately fired and shot the great chief through the breast, so that he fell forward into the water of the swamp, upon his face, dead. Philip was killed August 12th, 1676. Weetamoo's party, the sad remnant of her tribe, had been captured on the 7th, and she, trying to escape across a river, was drowned, and, her body being found, her head was cut off and paraded in the public streets. In the body of the papers, by a strange continuance of an old mistake, this fact is accredited to Awashonks, squaw sachem of the Sogkonates.

After Philip's death, his chief counsellor, Annawon, led the rest of the party out of the swamp and escaped. With his party he soon after surrendered to Mr. Church. The death of Philip was practically the close of the war, though hostilities continued for some time after, and at the eastward for a year or more longer. At Dover Major Richard Walderne had held command of the military interests and operations in those parts. He was a trusted friend of Wannalancet and the neighboring Indians. Under the proclamation the old chief and his people came in without fear, as they had taken no part whatever in the war. There were many Indians with them, however, it was suspected, who had been among the hostiles and now wished to come in with the Pennacooks and secure the advantages of their influence in giving themselves up. They began to come in at Dover about the first of September, and when, on the 6th, the companies, sent to the eastward under Capt. Hathorn, arrived at Dover, there were some four hundred there, including the Pennacooks. In some way the immediate surrender of all these was received, probably by Major Walderne's great influence with them. They were then disarmed, and as the Massachusetts officers insisted upon treating all as prisoners of war, Major Walderne was obliged to send all, save Wannalancet and his "relations," down to Boston to be tried there by the Court. The number sent was about two hundred.

Some of the Southern Indians, having lost all except their own lives, passed to the Eastern tribes and were active in exciting to hostility. The local Indians had been hostile the previous year, committing depredations from the Kennebec to Portsmouth. In the summer of 1676, it is thought that many who had been among the Indians in the war, came to these tribes and caused much of the trouble which ensued. The day before Philip's death the Indians fell upon the settlers at Falmouth, and killed or carried away some thirty-four persons and burned their houses. Further eastward also the settlements were attacked. It was upon these occasions that Capt. Hathorn's force was sent to these parts. They marched on from Dover on September 8th, as far as Falmouth, Capt. Hunting's Indians scouting the woods. This expedition was not of much avail, as the Indians easily eluded the troops, being only war parties without the encumbrance of women and children.

In November, 1676, a company was sent up into the mountain regions of New Hampshire to break up a winter encampment of the Ammoscoggin and Pigwacket Indians, who had been active in the hostile movements at the eastward settlements during the summer and fall, and were now said to be gathering into winter quarters in a great fort, near "Ossapy Lake."

After a severe march, the fort was discovered, but no signs of Indians, and after scouting in small parties some twelve miles beyond this fort, they burned the same, and marched back to Berwick, having been gone nine days. In the meantime the Penobscot sagamore, Mugg, or, as he was afterwards called, "Mogg Hegone" (and in Whittier's poem Mogg Megone), came to the English in behalf of Madockawando, the sachem of Penobscot, to treat for peace, and the return of the English captives. A treaty was concluded at Boston, November 6th, 1676, by which Mugg agreed to return all the captives and goods taken from the English, and offered to remain with the English until the same was done. Two vessels were fitted out, and sailed to Penobscot, where they arrived the first week in December, and found the great chief, Madockawando, who received and treated them kindly. He delivered to them two captives, who were then with him, and Mugg was allowed to go up into the country, to try to bring down some others, who were said to be at another camp. He did not return; and the vessels, after a few days' waiting, sailed to Pemaquid, where they received some more English captives, and returned home. Among the captives received at Pemaquid was Thomas Cobbet, son of Rev. Thomas, of Ipswich. He had been among the savages for several months, and his interesting story of his captivity gave much and correct information in regard to the strength, habits, temper, and intentions of the Indians and their other captives.

Soon after that, another captive, Francis Card, escaped and brought later news, and one item of great importance was that Mugg had returned to the Indians on the Kennebec, who were the real leaders in the war in those parts. He said that Mugg boasted greatly of the trick he had played upon the English, and threatened great things to be done against them in the spring. He gave a minute description of the country, the condition of the Indians, and the easiest approaches to their places of encampment.

He said that the numbers of the Indians were not so large as reported, their war-party, in full force, being not over a hundred men. The captives with them were well, and not abused, except they were made to work for their captors. Stirred up and encouraged by this report, the Council at Boston raised a force of two hundred men, of whom sixty were Natick Indians, and sent them away by water, to the eastward, the first week in February; Major Waldron, of Dover, being Commander-in-chief of the expedition. The forces were at Blackpoint on February 17th, and sailed eastward along the shore, landing in Maquoit Bay, where Capt. Frost with his company had a skirmish with a body of the savages, without much loss on either side, and followed next day with an attempt at a treaty. Thence they sailed around to the Kennebec, and landing at Arrowsick Island, left a part of their force there, to build a fort and establish a garrison. Major Waldron, with a part of the company under Capt. Frost, went to Pemaquid and ransomed some captives there; but, discovering a plot to destroy himself and a small party who went on shore to treat with the Indians, he called his soldiers ashore, and attacking the enemy furiously, drove them to their canoes which they had near by, killing some, among whom was the sagamore Mattahando, leader in this affair. Sailing back to Arrowsick, Major Waldron gathered his forces together, leaving a small garrison at Kennebec, and went home to Boston, where they arrived safely, without the loss of a man, on March 11th, 1677.

In April following an attempt was made by the Massachusetts authorities to enlist the Mohawk

Indians against the hostile savages upon the North and Eastern borders. Major Pynchon, of Springfield, with Mr. James Richards of Hartford, and twelve men as a guard, made a journey to the Mohawk country to arrange for their coöperation.

This action was taken with the advice of Gov. Andros, of New York, and some of the Indians did really come into the borders of New Hampshire and Maine; but the distance was so great from their country that little was achieved except by the terror inspired among the Eastern tribes, by the rumor of their coming.

This measure was questioned by many as to its lawfulness, in employing heathen to fight the battles of the Lord; but the General Court fell back upon the scriptural precedent of Abraham employing the Amorites, and so justified its somewhat questionable proceeding. The Indians on the Kennebec were not deterred from hostilities, which were renewed by the killing of nine of the garrison left the year before, at that place. So the Massachusetts Court at once called upon the other colonies to assist them in raising a new force to send into those parts. Up to the present time, Massachusetts had borne the whole expense of the Eastern wars, but now call them to raise their proportional part of one hundred English, and two hundred Indian soldiers, to rendezvous at Blackpoint. But in the meantime Massachusetts had acted with promptness in sending Capt. Hunting to bring the remaining garrison at Kennebec, and strengthening the garrisons at Wells with a company under Capt. Benjamin Swett, and at Blackpoint with another company under Lieut. Tippin. In May, the Eastern tribes, elated by their success in driving the English out of their country, gathered all their forces against the above garrisons. The Indian leaders in this campaign were Symon, a renegade Christian Indian, and Mugg, above mentioned, both wary and skilful, and well acquainted with the country around, and with the English people and their habits. The Indian forces under these leaders at this time were well-tried men from the Penobscot, Kennebec, and Ammoscoggin tribes of the Tarratines, ranking as fighters next to the Pequods and Mohawks. They were well equipped and supplied, probably by the French in Canada.

It does not appear that either of the other colonies sent men to assist in this campaign, and the force that was raised by Massachusetts was too small, and the English part of it was mostly of young and untried men and boys who had seen no service except in garrisons. They seem also to have entirely underrated the numbers and temper of the enemy. On the 13th of May, the Blackpoint garrison had beaten off a large body of the Indians after a fierce assault of three days, on the last of which Lieut. Tippin had shot and killed the leader, Mugg; when the Indians had gone away towards Wells and York, as told above. On July 28th, Capt. Swett, with forty young English recruits, and a company of thirty-six Natick Indians, landed at Blackpoint garrison-house, the Indians being under the command of Lieut. James Richardson. Next morning the enemy with quite a large party appeared not far from the fort, when Capt. Swett drew out his whole force, with a number from the garrison, and pursued them with headlong haste about two miles, when, at the edge of a hill, with a dark swamp on each side, they found themselves ambushed, after the old fashion at Brookfield, Deerfield, Sudbury, etc., whose lessons, after two centuries, the American soldiers have not fully learned. Half the English were shot down at the first volley, and the raw young lads were completely panicstricken, and unable to make any defence. The Captain with a few tried men rallied and attempted to bring off their wounded and make good a retreat to the fort. The odds were too heavy against him, and having received many wounds, he was at last surrounded and overpowered by the foe, and fell not far from the garrison, still fighting.

Lieut. Richardson fell near the first onset. Forty of the English and twelve of the Natick Indians were killed at the time. It is not known how many the enemy lost; but they made no further attempt upon the garrison and soon retired. The next hostile move of these Indians was in a new direction. They captured no less than thirteen fishing-vessels with their crews and loads along the Eastern shores.

In August of this year (1677), Gov. Andros, of New York, sent a ship with a force of men to Pemaquid, which, when the Indians understood, they soon, for some reason, came to proper terms of peace, returned the English captives and the captured vessels into the hands of the New York soldiers, by whom they were soon returned home.

Yet another act in this long tragedy was to come.

The scene changes to Hatfield, where, September 19th, the people of that village were engaged in raising a house, having no thought of any Indian hostility in the colony. Suddenly they were set upon by a party of River Indians, forty or fifty in number, who had crept about them so secretly that they were unarmed and utterly helpless. Some were shot down from the frame of the building. Twelve were killed outright, and some twenty more were made captive and carried to Canada. The story of the captivity and redemption of these last, by the two brave Hatfield men, Benjamin Wait and Stephen Jennings, is one of the most heroic and interesting of the whole war. The Indians killed one man and captured three more at Deerfield that same day. This was the last act of any considerable importance in the war known as "King Philip's War."

The Massinahigan Series:
Brief Accounts of Early Native America

For more information on this series, see our website at:
http://www.evolpub.com/Massinahigan/BAENA.html

www.ingramcontent.com/pod-product-compliance
Lightning Source LLC
Chambersburg PA
CBHW032107080426
42733CB00006B/455